INTRODUCTION

THE "EASY GUIDE TO DELETING PUBLIC RECORDS, INQUIRIES, AND EVICTIONS"!

IN THIS GUIDE, YOU'LL LEARN STRAIGHTFORWARD STEPS TO CLEAN UP YOUR CREDIT REPORT BY REMOVING PUBLIC RECORDS, INQUIRIES, AND EVICTIONS.

WE'LL ALSO COVER THE USE OF 609 LETTERS, A TOOL TO DISPUTE INACCURATE INFORMATION ON YOUR CREDIT REPORT.

LET'S GET STARTED!

CONTENTS

01
PUBLIC RECORDS

02
INQUIRIES

03
EVICTIONS

"Easy Guide to Removing Public Records, Inquiries, and Evictions"

WHAT ARE PUBLIC RECORDS?

PUBLIC RECORDS INCLUDE BANKRUPTCIES, TAX LIENS, JUDGMENTS, AND OTHER LEGAL FILINGS THAT CAN APPEAR ON YOUR CREDIT REPORT. THESE RECORDS CAN NEGATIVELY IMPACT YOUR CREDIT SCORE AND FINANCIAL WELL-BEING.

WHAT IS A EVICTION?

EVICTIONS ARE COURT ORDERS TO LEAVE A RENTAL PROPERTY DUE TO NON-PAYMENT OR LEASE VIOLATIONS. EVICTIONS CAN STAY ON YOUR CREDIT REPORT AND AFFECT YOUR ABILITY TO RENT IN THE FINANCIAL FUTURE.

WHAT ARE INQUIRIES?

CREDIT INQUIRIES ARE RECORDS OF COMPANIES OR INDIVIDUALS WHO HAVE ACCESSED YOUR CREDIT REPORT. TOO MANY INQUIRIES CAN SUGGEST RISK TO LENDERS AND LOWER YOUR CREDIT SCORE.

CHAPTER 1: PUBLIC RECORDS

WHAT ARE PUBLIC RECORDS?

PUBLIC RECORDS ARE LEGAL FILINGS THAT ARE ACCESSIBLE TO THE PUBLIC. THEY INCLUDE BANKRUPTCY, TAX LIENS, JUDGMENTS, COURT FILINGS AND MORE.

FOR EXAMPLE, IF THERE'S A FORECLOSURE ON YOUR CREDIT REPORT OR A JUDGEMENT GRANTED, THIS INFORMATION CAN BE FOUND ON YOUR CREDIT REORT. THIS CAN GIVE THE WRONG IMPRESSION ABOUT YOUR FINANCIAL RESPONSIBILITY OR LEGAL HISTORY.

IMPACT ON YOUR CREDIT

PUBLIC RECORDS CAN SIGNIFICANTLY LOWER YOUR CREDIT SCORE AND MAKE IT HARDER TO GET APPROVED FOR LOANS OR CREDIT CARDS.

CREDIT BUREAUS ARE REQUIRED BY LAW TO VERIFY THE ACCURACY OF PUBLIC RECORDS REPORTED ON CREDIT FILES.

THIS MAY INVOLVE SEEKING ALTERNATIVE SOURCES OF VERIFICATION TO CONFIRM THE ACCURACY OF PUBLIC RECORDS. IF THERE'S A DISCREPANCY OR LACK OF VERIFICATION DUE TO COURT DENIAL, CONSUMERS HAVE THE RIGHT TO DISPUTE THE INFORMATION WITH THE CREDIT BUREAUS AND REQUEST FURTHER INVESTIGATION.

IDENTITY THEFT:

IF THE PUBLIC RECORDS ARE THE RESULT OF IDENTITY THEFT, FILE A POLICE REPORT AND PROVIDE TO CREDIT BUREAUS.

FILE A FTC REPORT

FILING AN IDENTITY THEFT REPORT WITH THE FTC CAN BE A CRUCIAL STEP IN PROTECTING YOUR CREDIT. IT PROVES YOU'RE A VICTIM OF IDENTITY THEFT AND ALLOWS YOU TO PLACE A FRAUD ALERT OR FREEZE ON YOUR CREDIT REPORTS.

THIS MAKES IT HARDER FOR IDENTITY THIEVES TO OPEN NEW ACCOUNTS USING YOUR IDENTITY.

PROVIDING THE IDENTITY THEFT REPORT TO CREDIT BUREAUS CAN HELP IN REMOVING FRAUDULENT ACCOUNTS OR TRANSACTIONS FROM YOUR CREDIT REPORT, RESTORING YOUR CREDIT TO ITS ACCURATE STATE.

FOR IDENTITY THEFT ISSUES, YOU'LL WANT TO FILE A COMPLAINT WITH BOTH THE CONSUMER FINANCIAL PROTECTION BUREAU (CFPB) AND THE FEDERAL TRADE COMMISSION (FTC). THE FTC HANDLES IDENTITY THEFT COMPLAINTS AND PROVIDES RESOURCES TO HELP YOU RECOVER FROM IDENTITY THEFT, WHILE THE CFPB CAN ASSIST WITH RELATED FINANCIAL ISSUES, SUCH AS UNAUTHORIZED CHARGES OR FRAUDULENT ACCOUNTS. IT'S A GOOD IDEA TO FILE WITH BOT!

BELOW I HAVE PROVIDE THE CONTACT INFORMATION FOR YOU TO PROCEED WITH SECURING YOUR CREDIT PROFILE.

FTC (FEDERAL TRADE COMMISSION):

- WEBSITE: WWW.FTC.GOV
- PHONE NUMBER: 1-877-FTC-HELP (1-877-382-4357)

CFPB (CONSUMER FINANCIAL PROTECTION BUREAU):

- WEBSITE: WWW.CONSUMERFINANCE.GOV
- PHONE NUMBER: 1-855-411-CFPB (1-855-411-2372)

HOW TO REMOVE PUBLIC RECORDS

STEP 1:
CHECK FOR ERRORS

1. OBTAIN YOUR CREDIT REPORTS: GET COPIES OF YOUR CREDIT REPORTS FROM EQUIFAX, EXPERIAN, AND TRANSUNION. YOU'RE ENTITLED TO A FREE REPORT FROM EACH BUREAU ONCE A YEAR AT ANNUALCREDITREPORT.COM.

2. REVIEW FOR INACCURACIES:

LOOK FOR ANY ERRORS IN THE PUBLIC RECORDS SECTION. THIS COULD INCLUDE INCORRECT DATES, AMOUNTS, OR DETAILS.

STEP 2:
DISPUTE INACCURATE RECORDS

WRITE A DISPUTE LETTER:

CREATE A FORMAL DISPUTE LETTER TO THE CREDIT BUREAUS (EQUIFAX, EXPERIAN, TRANSUNION) EXPLAINING THE INACCURACIES.

STEP 3:
SEND THE DISPUTE LETTER

MAIL THE DISPUTE LETTERS:

SEND THE DISPUTE LETTERS VIA CERTIFIED MAIL WITH RETURN RECEIPT REQUESTED TO ENSURE THEY RECEIVE IT.

FOLLOW UP:

KEEP RECORDS OF WHEN YOU SENT THE LETTERS AND ANY RESPONSES YOU RECEIVE. THE CREDIT BUREAUS HAVE 30 DAYS TO INVESTIGATE YOUR DISPUTE.

IT IS THE CREDIT BUREAUS DUTY TO GET PHYSICAL PROOF AND PROVIDE YOU WITH A COPY OF WHAT IS IN YOUR FILE THAT VERIFIED THIS DEBT. IF THEY CANT PROVIDE PROOF YOU NEED TO REQUEST THEY DELETE THE DEBT.

IF THE CREDIT BUREAU CONTINUES TO VERIFY INFORMATION WITHOUT PROVIDING PROOF, YOUR NEXT STEP WOULD BE TO ESCALATE THE DISPUTE.

FILE A COMPLAINT WITH THE CFPB WHEN YOU HAVE ISSUES WITH FINANCIAL PRODUCTS OR SERVICES, LIKE ERRORS ON YOUR CREDIT REPORT, UNAUTHORIZED CHARGES, DEBT COLLECTION PROBLEMS, OR ISSUES WITH LOANS OR MORTGAGES.

IF THE CONSUMER FINANCIAL PROTECTION BUREAU (CFPB) FINDS THAT A CREDIT BUREAU HAS VIOLATED THE FAIR CREDIT REPORTING ACT (FCRA), THEY CAN TAKE VARIOUS ACTIONS. THIS MIGHT INCLUDE FINES, REQUIRING THE CREDIT BUREAU TO CORRECT THE ERRORS, OR EVEN TAKING LEGAL ACTION IF NECESSARY. THEIR GOAL IS TO ENFORCE THE FCRA AND ENSURE FAIR AND ACCURATE CREDIT REPORTING.

4. INCLUDE EVIDENCE:

PROVIDE ANY SUPPORTING DOCUMENTS THAT PROVE THE INFORMATION IS WRONG. THIS COULD BE COURT DOCUMENTS, LETTERS, OR STATEMENTS.

DONT GIVE UP!

IF THE FIRST ROUND DONT SUCCED REQUEST THAT THE CREDIT BUREAU RE-INVESTIGATE THE INFORMATION.

SAMPLE TEMPLATE DISPUTE LETTER 1:

[YOUR NAME]
[YOUR ADDRESS]
[CITY, STATE ZIP CODE]
[DATE]

[CREDIT BUREAU NAME]
[ADDRESS]
[CITY, STATE ZIP CODE]

DEAR SIR/MADAM,

I AM WRITING TO DISPUTE THE FOLLOWING PUBLIC RECORD ON MY CREDIT REPORT:

- [PUBLIC RECORD DESCRIPTION: BANKRUPTCY, TAX LIEN, JUDGMENT, ETC.]
- [ACCOUNT NUMBER OR REFERENCE NUMBER, IF AVAILABLE]

I BELIEVE THIS PUBLIC RECORD IS INACCURATE. PLEASE INVESTIGATE AND REMOVE THIS INFORMATION FROM MY CREDIT REPORT AS SOON AS POSSIBLE.

ENCLOSED ARE COPIES OF [SUPPORTING DOCUMENTS: COURT DOCUMENTS, LETTERS, ETC.] THAT SUPPORT MY DISPUTE.

SINCERELY,
[YOUR NAME]

SAMPLE TEMPLATE DISPUTE LETTER 2:

[YOUR NAME]
[YOUR ADDRESS]
[CITY, STATE, ZIP CODE]
[YOUR EMAIL ADDRESS]
[YOUR PHONE NUMBER]
[DATE]

[CREDIT BUREAU NAME]
[CREDIT BUREAU ADDRESS]
[CITY, STATE, ZIP CODE]

SUBJECT: REQUEST FOR REMOVAL OF PUBLIC RECORDS FROM CREDIT REPORT

DEAR SIR/MADAM,

I AM WRITING TO YOU REGARDING THE PUBLIC RECORDS LISTED ON MY CREDIT REPORT. ACCORDING TO THE FAIR CREDIT REPORTING ACT (FCRA), SPECIFICALLY SECTIONS 609 AND 611, CONSUMERS HAVE THE RIGHT TO DISPUTE INACCURATE INFORMATION ON THEIR CREDIT REPORTS.

UPON REVIEWING MY CREDIT REPORT, I HAVE NOTICED THE PRESENCE OF CERTAIN PUBLIC RECORDS THAT I BELIEVE ARE INACCURATE AND SHOULD BE REMOVED. THESE RECORDS ARE NEGATIVELY IMPACTING MY CREDITWORTHINESS AND FINANCIAL STANDING.

CONTINUED…

FURTHERMORE, I WOULD LIKE TO BRING TO YOUR ATTENTION THAT THE CONSUMER FINANCIAL PROTECTION BUREAU (CFPB) ENFORCES LAWS TO ENSURE FAIR AND ACCURATE CREDIT REPORTING. AS SUCH, I AM EXERCISING MY RIGHTS UNDER BOTH THE FCRA AND CFPB LAWS TO REQUEST THE REMOVAL OF THE FOLLOWING PUBLIC RECORDS FROM MY CREDIT REPORT:

1. [SPECIFY THE NATURE OF THE PUBLIC RECORD, SUCH AS A BANKRUPTCY, TAX LIEN, JUDGMENT, ETC.]
2. [INCLUDE ANY ADDITIONAL PUBLIC RECORDS THAT ARE INACCURATE OR OUTDATED]

I AM REQUESTING A THOROUGH INVESTIGATION INTO THESE PUBLIC RECORDS AND URGE YOU TO TAKE APPROPRIATE ACTION TO REMOVE ANY INFORMATION THAT CANNOT BE VERIFIED OR IS NOT IN COMPLIANCE WITH THE FCRA AND CFPB REGULATIONS.

CONTINUED…

ENCLOSED ARE COPIES OF SUPPORTING DOCUMENTS THAT VALIDATE MY CLAIMS AND SUBSTANTIATE THE INACCURACIES IN THE PUBLIC RECORDS MENTIONED ABOVE.

THANK YOU FOR YOUR PROMPT ATTENTION TO THIS MATTER.

SINCERELY,
[YOUR NAME]

ENCLOSURES: [LIST OF ENCLOSED DOCUMENTS, IF ANY]

 FILL IN THE BLANKS:

HANDWRITE ALL PERSONAL AND ACCOUNT INFORMATION.

HANDWRITING THE FILL-IN BLANKS IN YOUR DISPUTE LETTER CAN INDEED INCREASE THE LIKELIHOOD OF YOUR LETTER BEING REVIEWED BY A REAL PERSON RATHER THAN PROCESSED BY AUTOMATED SYSTEMS. THIS PERSONAL TOUCH CAN POTENTIALLY LEAD TO A MORE THOROUGH INVESTIGATION OF YOUR DISPUTE AND A MORE EFFECTIVE RESOLUTION.

CHAPTER 2: INQUIRIES

AN INQUIRY ON YOUR CREDIT REPORT HAPPENS WHEN SOMEONE, LIKE A LENDER OR CREDITOR, CHECKS YOUR CREDIT HISTORY.

THIS USUALLY OCCURS WHEN YOU APPLY FOR CREDIT, LIKE A LOAN OR CREDIT CARD.

THERE ARE TWO TYPES:

"HARD" INQUIRIES, WHICH HAPPEN WHEN YOU APPLY FOR CREDIT.

"SOFT" INQUIRIES, WHICH OCCUR WHEN A COMPANY CHECKS YOUR CREDIT FOR PROMOTIONAL OFFERS OR BACKGROUND CHECKS, AND DON'T AFFECT YOUR CREDIT SCORE.

Too many inquiries can make lenders cautious because they indicate that you've recently applied for credit, potentially signaling financial stress or a high desire for credit.

While individual inquiries typically have a minimal impact on your credit score (usually a few points), multiple inquiries within a short period, especially for different types of credit, can have a more significant effect.

The impact of inquiries on your score diminishes after about a year, they no longer affect your score.

TO MINIMIZE CREDIT INQUIRIES WHILE SEEKING NEW CREDIT, CONSIDER THESE STRATEGIES:

1. RESEARCH BEFORE APPLYING:

PRIORITIZE LENDERS THAT OFFER PRE-QUALIFICATION OPTIONS, WHICH ALLOW YOU TO CHECK YOUR ELIGIBILITY WITHOUT A HARD INQUIRY AFFECTING YOUR CREDIT SCORE.

2. LIMIT APPLICATIONS:

ONLY APPLY FOR CREDIT WHEN YOU'RE CONFIDENT YOU MEET THE REQUIREMENTS AND INTEND TO PROCEED WITH THE APPLICATION.

3. TIME APPLICATIONS STRATEGICALLY:

Space out credit applications over time to avoid multiple inquiries within a short period, which can raise red flags for lenders.

4. FOCUS ON TARGETED APPLICATIONS:

Apply for credit only when necessary and avoid submitting numerous applications for different types of credit simultaneously.

5. CONSIDER ALTERNATIVES:

Explore options like credit unions or local banks that may offer personalized services and be more lenient with inquiries.

TO DELETE AN INQUIRY FROM YOUR CREDIT REPORT, YOU CAN DISPUTE IT WITH THE CREDIT BUREAUS.

WRITE A LETTER OR SUBMIT A DISPUTE ONLINE, EXPLAINING WHY THE INQUIRY IS INCORRECT OR UNAUTHORIZED.

THE CREDIT BUREAU WILL INVESTIGATE, AND IF THEY CAN'T VERIFY THE INQUIRY, THEY'LL REMOVE IT FROM YOUR REPORT.

REMEMBER TO INCLUDE ANY SUPPORTING DOCUMENTS, LIKE PROOF OF IDENTITY THEFT IF THAT'S THE CASE.

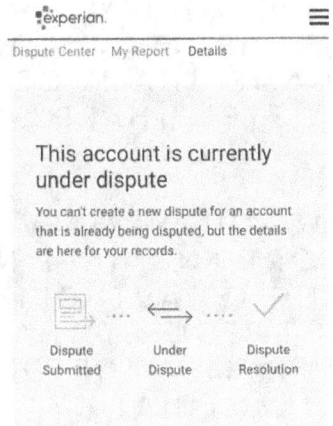

SAMPLE LETTER TEMPLATE

[YOUR NAME]
[YOUR ADDRESS]
[CITY, STATE, ZIP CODE]
[DATE]

[CREDIT BUREAU NAME]
[CREDIT BUREAU ADDRESS]
[CITY, STATE, ZIP CODE]

SUBJECT: DISPUTE OF UNAUTHORIZED CREDIT INQUIRIES

Dear Sir/Madam,

I am writing to dispute the following unauthorized credit inquiries listed on my credit report:

1. INQUIRY DATE: [DATE]
CREDITOR NAME: [NAME OF CREDITOR]
INQUIRY TYPE: [HARD OR SOFT INQUIRY]

2. INQUIRY DATE: [DATE]
CREDITOR NAME: [NAME OF CREDITOR]
INQUIRY TYPE: [HARD OR SOFT INQUIRY]

I have thoroughly reviewed my credit report and have no record of initiating or authorizing these inquiries. I request that they be removed from my credit report immediately.

CONTINUED…

Enclosed are copies of supporting documentation, including correspondence with the respective creditors, demonstrating that these inquiries were unauthorized. Additionally, I have included proof of my identity to facilitate the investigation process.

According to the Fair Credit Reporting Act (FCRA), consumers have the right to dispute inaccurate or unauthorized information on their credit reports. I trust that you will conduct a thorough investigation into this matter and take appropriate action to rectify the inaccuracies.

Please provide me with written confirmation once the unauthorized inquiries have been removed from my credit report.

Thank you for your prompt attention to this matter.

Sincerely,

[Your Name]

Enclosures: [List of enclosed documents, such as copies of supporrting documentation and proof of identity]

FILL IN THE BLANKS:

HANDWRITE ALL PERSONAL AND ACCOUNT INFORMATION.

HANDWRITING THE FILL-IN BLANKS IN YOUR DISPUTE LETTER CAN INDEED INCREASE THE LIKELIHOOD OF YOUR LETTER BEING REVIEWED BY A REAL PERSON RATHER THAN PROCESSED BY AUTOMATED SYSTEMS. THIS PERSONAL TOUCH CAN POTENTIALLY LEAD TO A MORE THOROUGH INVESTIGATION OF YOUR DISPUTE AND A MORE EFFECTIVE RESOLUTION.

CHAPTER 3: EVICTIONS

An eviction can end up on your credit report if your landlord or property management company reports the eviction to one or more of the major credit bureaus (Equifax, Experian, or TransUnion). Landlords may report evictions to credit bureaus as way to collecting unpaid rent or damages owed.

When trying to remove evictions from your credit report, you'll want to reference the Fair Credit Reporting Act (FCRA), specifically:

- Section 609(a)(1):

This section requires credit bureaus to provide accurate and complete information to consumers, including evictions.

- SECTION 623(A)(1)(A):

THIS SECTION REQUIRES THAT INFORMATION REPORTED TO CREDIT BUREAUS MUST BE ACCURATE AND MUST BE CORRECTED OR DELETED IF FOUND TO BE INACCURATE OR INCOMPLETE.

IF YOU'RE TRYING TO REMOVE EVICTIONS FROM YOUR CREDIT REPORT, YOU CAN USE A "609 LETTER" AS A FORMAL REQUEST TO THE CREDIT BUREAUS.

SAMPLE LETTER TEMPLATE:

[YOUR NAME]
[YOUR ADDRESS]
[CITY, STATE, ZIP CODE]
[DATE]

[CREDIT BUREAU NAME]
[CREDIT BUREAU ADDRESS]
[CITY, STATE, ZIP CODE]

SUBJECT: REQUEST FOR INVESTIGATION AND REMOVAL OF INACCURATE EVICTION INFORMATION

DEAR SIR OR MADAM,

I AM WRITING TO DISPUTE THE EVICTION INFORMATION ON MY CREDIT REPORT. ACCORDING TO MY RECORDS, THERE IS INACCURATE INFORMATION REGARDING AN EVICTION LISTED UNDER [SPECIFY THE ACCOUNT NUMBER OR DESCRIPTION OF THE EVICTION].

CONTINUED…

I believe this eviction information is incorrect because [explain the reason, such as the eviction never occurred, it was resolved, etc.]. I have attached supporting documents [if available, such as a court dismissal, proof of payment, or a letter from the landlord] to verify this.

I am requesting that this eviction information be promptly investigated and removed from my credit report in accordance with the Fair Credit Reporting Act (FCRA), particularly under Section 609(a)(1) and Section 623(a)(1)(A).

Please provide me with written confirmation once this investigation is completed and the eviction has been removed from my credit report.

Thank you for your prompt attention to this matter.

Sincerely,
[Your Name]

IF THE COURT DID NOT GRANT JUDGMENT IN THE COLLECTION OF RENT AND THE EVICTION IS STILL ON YOUR PUBLIC RECORD, YOU MAY HAVE GROUNDS TO HAVE IT REMOVED.

1. REVIEW THE COURT RECORDS:

OBTAIN A COPY OF THE COURT RECORDS RELATED TO THE EVICTION CASE. VERIFY THAT THERE WAS NO JUDGMENT ISSUED AGAINST YOU FOR THE COLLECTION OF RENT.

2. CONTACT THE COURT:

REACH OUT TO THE COURT CLERK'S OFFICE WHERE THE EVICTION CASE WAS FILED. INQUIRE ABOUT THE PROCESS FOR HAVING THE EVICTION REMOVED FROM PUBLIC RECORDS IF NO JUDGMENT WAS GRANTED.

3. FILE A MOTION TO EXPUNGE OR SEAL:

DEPENDING ON THE LAWS IN YOUR JURISDICTION, YOU MAY BE ABLE TO FILE A MOTION TO EXPUNGE OR SEAL THE EVICTION FROM PUBLIC RECORDS SINCE THERE WAS NO JUDGMENT ISSUED. FOLLOW THE PROCEDURES OUTLINED BY THE COURT FOR THIS PROCESS.

IF THE COURTS DID NOT GRANT A JUDGMENT FOR THE COLLECTION OF RENT IN COURT, IT SUGGESTS THAT THE EVICTION PROCESS MAY NOT HAVE BEEN COMPLETED OR FINALIZED.

DISPUTE, DISPUTE, AND CONTINUE TO DISPUTE.

AN EVICTION RESULTING FROM IDENTITY THEFT?

1. CONTACT THE LANDLORD:

REACH OUT TO THE LANDLORD OR PROPERTY MANAGEMENT COMPANY WHO REPORTED THE EVICTION. EXPLAIN THE SITUATION AND PROVIDE THEM WITH DOCUMENTATION PROVING THAT THE EVICTION WAS A RESULT OF IDENTITY THEFT. REQUEST THAT THEY RETRACT THE EVICTION FROM YOUR RECORD.

2. DISPUTE WITH CREDIT BUREAUS:

SUBMIT A DISPUTE TO THE CREDIT BUREAUS (EQUIFAX, EXPERIAN, AND TRANSUNION) STATING THAT THE EVICTION WAS THE RESULT OF IDENTITY THEFT. INCLUDE COPIES OF THE POLICE REPORT AND ANY OTHER SUPPORTING DOCUMENTATION. REQUEST THAT THEY INVESTIGATE AND REMOVE THE EVICTION FROM YOUR CREDIT REPORT.

BY DISPUTING THE EVICTION, YOU AIM TO HAVE IT REMOVED FROM YOUR RECORD ENTIRELY, WHICH CAN HAVE A MORE SIGNIFICANT POSITIVE IMPACT ON YOUR CREDIT HISTORY AND FUTURE RENTAL PROSPECTS.

SETTLEMENT, ON THE OTHER HAND, TYPICALLY INVOLVES PAYING THE DEBT ASSOCIATED WITH THE EVICTION BUT MAY NOT RESULT IN ITS REMOVAL FROM YOUR RECORD, POTENTIALLY STILL AFFECTING YOUR CREDIT AND RENTAL OPPORTUNITIES.

VALIDATION OF DEBT
ACCOUNT NUMBER: [YOUR ACCOUNT NUMBER]

Dear Sir/Madam,

I am writing to dispute the accuracy of information on my credit report regarding the account referenced above. According to Section 609 of the Fair Credit Reporting Act, I am requesting validation of this debt.

Please provide the following information:

1. The original signed contract or application.
2. The complete account history, including all statements.
3. Proof of the statute of limitations.

If you are unable to provide this information, I request that the item be removed from my credit report.

Sincerely,

[PRINT NAME]

HERE ARE THE STATUTES OF LIMITATIONS FOR REPORTING DEBTS ON CREDIT REPORTS IN ALL 50 STATES:

1. ALABAMA: 3 YEARS
2. ALASKA: 6 YEARS
3. ARIZONA: 6 YEARS
4. ARKANSAS: 5 YEARS
5. CALIFORNIA: 7 YEARS
6. COLORADO: 7 YEARS
7. CONNECTICUT: 7 YEARS
8. DELAWARE: 3 YEARS
9. FLORIDA: 5 YEARS
10. GEORGIA: 6 YEARS
11. HAWAII: 6 YEARS
12. IDAHO: 5 YEARS
13. ILLINOIS: 7 YEARS
14. INDIANA: 7 YEARS
15. IOWA: 5 YEARS
16. KANSAS: 5 YEARS
17. KENTUCKY: 5 YEARS
18. LOUISIANA: 3 YEARS
19. MAINE: 6 YEARS
20. MARYLAND: 3 YEARS
21. MASSACHUSETTS: 6 YEARS
22. MICHIGAN: 6 YEARS
23. MINNESOTA: 6 YEARS
24. MISSISSIPPI: 3 YEARS
25. MISSOURI: 5 YEARS
26. MONTANA: 8 YEARS

CONTINUED ON NEXT PAGE…

27. NEBRASKA: 5 YEARS
28. NEVADA: 6 YEARS
29. NEW HAMPSHIRE: 3 YEARS
30. NEW JERSEY: 6 YEARS
31. NEW MEXICO: 4 YEARS
32. NEW YORK: 6 YEARS
33. NORTH CAROLINA: 5 YEARS
34. NORTH DAKOTA: 6 YEARS
35. OHIO: 6 YEARS
36. OKLAHOMA: 5 YEARS
37. OREGON: 6 YEARS
38. PENNSYLVANIA: 4 YEARS
39. RHODE ISLAND: 10 YEARS
40. SOUTH CAROLINA: 7 YEARS
41. SOUTH DAKOTA: 6 YEARS
42. TENNESSEE: 6 YEARS
43. TEXAS: 4 YEARS
44. UTAH: 6 YEARS
45. VERMONT: 6 YEARS
46. VIRGINIA: 5 YEARS
47. WASHINGTON: 7 YEARS
48. WEST VIRGINIA: 5 YEARS
49. WISCONSIN: 6 YEARS
50. WYOMING: 8 YEARS

THESE STATUTES OF LIMITATIONS REFER TO THE LENGTH OF TIME A DEBT CAN REMAIN ON YOUR CREDIT REPORT. AFTER THIS TIME PERIOD, THE DEBT SHOULD NO LONGER APPEAR ON YOUR CREDIT REPORT, THOUGH IT MAY STILL BE LEGALLY COLLECTIBLE.

Lenders view public records negatively, and having them on your report can make it harder to get approved for credit. Removing them makes you appear more creditworthy.

Lower Risk Perception:

Without public records, creditors may see you as less of a risk, potentially leading to better interest rates and terms on new credit.

By using the information provided to dispute and potentially remove public record and evictions, you can work towards a healthier credit report and a higher credit score.

This will now open up more opportunities for favorable credit offers in the future.

Regularly check your credit reports to see if the public records have been removed.

BIOGRAPHY

"IN THIS EMPOWERING EBOOK, I'VE SHARED WITH YOU THE KEYS TO UNLOCK A WORLD OF FINANCIAL FREEDOM AND PROSPERITY.

AS A SEASONED EXPERT IN THE REALM OF CREDIT MANAGEMENT, I'VE DEDICATED MY CAREER TO GUIDING INDIVIDUALS LIKE YOU TOWARDS A BRIGHTER FINANCIAL FUTURE.

GET READY TO EMBARK ON A JOURNEY OF SELF-DISCOVERY, EMPOWERMENT, AND LASTING PROSPERITY."

—ANTONIONIA MARIE

www.ingramcontent.com/pod-product-compliance
Lightning Source LLC
Chambersburg PA
CBHW071203240526
45470CB00017B/1247